OTHER HELEN EXLEY GIFTBOOKS:

Sisters...
To a very special Sister
The Love Between Sisters
In Celebration of Women
A Special Collection in Praise of Mothers
The Love Between Friends
My Daughter My Joy
The Love Between Grandmothers and Grandchildren

Published simultaneously in 1998 by Exley Publications Ltd in Great Britain and
Exley Publications LLC in the USA.

4   6   8   10   12   11   9   7   5   3

Selection and arrangement copyright © Helen Exley 1998.
The moral right of the author has been asserted.

ISBN 1-86187-164-3

My thanks to Pam Brown for her writing and invaluable help with this book.
And, again, my thanks to Margaret Montgomery for helping me with the research.
I'd like also to take this opportunity to thank my team for their support
in preparing this book. – *Helen.*
Words and pictures selected by Helen Exley.
Border illustrations by Angela Kerr.
Pictures researched by Image Select International.
Printed in China.

Exley Publications Ltd, 16 Chalk Hill, Watford, Herts WD19 4BG, UK.
Exley Publications LLC, 232 Madison Avenue, Suite 1409, NY 10016, USA.

IN PRAISE *AND CELEBRATION OF*

Sisters

A H E L E N E X L E Y G I F T B O O K

EXLEY
NEW YORK • WATFORD, UK

I have always loved my sister's voice. It is clear and light, a voice without seasons.... Her voice is a greening thing, an enemy of storm and dark and winter.

TOM WINGO, FOR HIS TWIN SISTER SAVANNAH

Irene wasn't only beautiful. She had a wonderful charm.... When she came in, it was like the sun streaming into the room.

NANCY LANGHORNE, LATER LADY ASTOR

Her presence makes the room warm and alive for me. I want to be where she is. It is not a very conscious feeling – just a vague discontent with the places where she is not. There is more life where she is. I get up and follow her when she moves from one room to another as one might unconsciously follow a moving patch of sunlight in a room.

ANNE MORROW LINDBERGH, ON HER SISTER ELIZABETH

... I had a friend. Someone to wake up to in the mornings. Someone to laugh with. Someone to pinch and to punch and to tell tales to, and about. Someone to get into trouble with. Someone to share the blame and the blows, and the secrets. Someone to whisper with, to wink at, to pull faces to behind the backs of the grown-ups. Someone to dream with, to share plans for the future. Someone to hold hands with, to nudge in chapel, and to kick under the tea-table. Someone to complain to about parental unfairness. Someone to steal jelly with, and jam, and spoonfuls of honey out of the larder. Someone to throw a ball to, and hold a skipping rope, to race and to swim, and play snakes-and-ladders with. Above all, someone who shared my blackish sense of humour, who burst into fits of uncontrollable laughter, especially in the face of adversity. That was the very best thing about my sister. She was a giggler, like me.

MOLLY PARKIN

Sisters share the scent and smells
– the feel of a common childhood.
Hot raspberry jelly steaming in a bowl.
Uncooked currant cake.
Milk with a dash of coffee.
Crab apples and compost.
Dad's tweed jacket.
The pattern on the carpet.
The horsehair rasp of Grandma's sofa.
The bedroom curtains shining with the summer sun.
Cod liver oil and malt.
And licorice bootlaces.
We share a territory –
You and I.

PAM BROWN, b.1928

A sister is a little bit of childhood that can never be lost.

MARION C. GARRETTY

WHAT IS A SISTER?

She is your mirror, shining back at you with a world of possibilities.
She is your witness, who sees you at your worst and best, and loves you anyway. She is your partner in crime, your midnight companion, someone who knows when you are smiling, even in the dark. She is your teacher, your defense attorney, your personal press agent, even your shrink. Some days, she's the reason you wish you were an only child.

BARBARA ALPERT

Siblings are the people we practice on,

the people who teach us about fairness and

cooperation and kindness and caring –

quite often the hard way.

And that someone need not be perfect for

you to love them.

PAMELA DUGDALE

Dear Mum

I am writing to you to ask you if you could make my sister be quiet for a few seconds. Now I see why her nickname is Foghorn Fanny, with her loud music. I don't mind you teaching her drama, but could you make her a miming expert – you know, the stuff without words. And then you wonder why there are no birds in the garden. But the worst thing is at night when you put her to bed, you put me to bed too.

Love from Robbie.

ROBBIE JARVIS, AGED SEVEN

Growing up was a bit funny. Here we were together, messing about with buckets and earth, filling urns and pots, talking to each other as we had in the days of childhood. Comfortable in each other's company, knowing it so well, trusting it so deeply, relaxed, continuing. Aware that we knew each other better than perhaps anyone else would ever do. Conscious of each other's doubts, apprehension, and private joys, which were not private between us, because one flick of an eye, caught suddenly in a crowded place, amid laughter or conversation, struck instant, private responses which no one else on earth could ever share, and comforted us. Here I was at fifty-five. No longer the skinny boy in plimsolls and baggy shorts, and she no longer the thin child in a cotton dress and sandals... the exteriors had altered, but the minds, and above all, the affection, had stayed constant.

We remained the original children, on our own together; while all about us had quite altered.

DIRK BOGARDE, FROM "AN ORDERLY MAN"

The bond between us was not made from flowers and loving sentiments – but sitting on each other's heads, borrowing each other's things, arguing in whispers in the early hours. From secrets, silly and serious, that had to be kept from Mum. From last minute coaching for examinations – resentful and desperate. From shoutings and tears. From gigglings and raucous laughter. From plottings and from dire and dreadful threats and warnings.

We are grown now, established – but still I hear your voice in memory.

"Oh, don't be so ridiculous!"

"Don't be so wimpish. Stand up for yourself."

"Think!"

"Sleep on it."

"Cheer up, old love. Be brave, I'm right behind you."

And you are. Always.

PAM BROWN, b.1928

... loving a sister
is an unconditional,
narcissistic, and
complicated devotion that
approximates a mother's
love.... Sisters are
inescapably connected by
the same two parents, the
same trove of memory
and experience.

MARY BRUNO

*S*mall siblings let you tie their hair in tiny plaits all over
and dress them up like dolls. But, too, they give you hugs and sticky kisses
and cry if scolded, and climb into your bed when they are frightened,
and give you gifts – frogs and snails and dandelions
and squares of melting chocolate
... And teach you how to love.

PAMELA DUGDALE

A younger sister is someone to use as guinea-pig in trying sledges
and experimental go-carts.
Someone to send on messages to Mum.
But someone who needs you – who comes to you with bumped heads,
grazed knees, tales of persecution.
Someone who trusts you to defend her.
Someone who thinks you know the answers to almost everything.

PAM BROWN, b.1928

Older sisters... are liable to nag. To refuse to lend you things. To scold. To make you walk too fast.

But, on the other hand, they take on bully boys at school and send them running for their lives. They disentangle problems in arithmetic and knitting.

And when they're grown they listen to your secrets and anxieties. And never tell – without your say-so.

An older sister is a friend, and a defender – a listener, conspirator, a counsellor and a sharer of delights. And sorrows too.

PAM BROWN

For when three sisters love each other with such

sincere affection, the one does not experience sorrow,

pain, or affliction of any kind,

but the others' heart wishes to relieve, and

vibrates in tenderness.

Like a well-organized musical instrument.

ELIZABETH SHAW, SISTER OF ABIGAIL ADAMS AND MARY CRANCH

We're just women who admire and really know each other. We allow each other to have the weaknesses the public doesn't allow us to have....

LIZA MINELLI

Whatever you do they will love you; even if they don't love you they are connected till you die. You can be boring and tedious with sisters, whereas you have to put on a good face with friends.

DEBORAH MOGGACH

We have quarrelled, I know –
when someone kept knocking down the tower of bricks.
When someone went on singing while
the other tried to sleep.
When someone picked out all the chocolate biscuits.
We squabbled, I know –
over whose turn it was to scrape the cake mix bowl,
and who had taken the other's bike.
But it gave life an extra interest, didn't it?
And when there was an excitement, an adventure,
a surprise – we shared it.
And when there was a sadness, we shared that too.
Life alone would have been tidier and less fraught –
but without astonishments,
without plots and plans,
without sympathetic hugs.
Life without a sister would have been
far more lonely – and far, far more dull.

TONI LEVI

Sugar and spice and all things nice.
Perhaps. To an outsider.
… Siblings are more realistic. To them a
sister is naggings and needlings, whispers
and whisperings. Bribery. Thumpings.

Borrowings. Breakings.
Kisses and cuddlings. Lendings. Surprises.
Defendings and comfortings.
Welcomings home.

PAM BROWN

Sisters are inclined to moan about each other to their closest relatives.

"She's always been like that."

"Why doesn't she ever learn?"

"I told her so."

"That girl's a fool to herself."

"If only...."

But let an outsider offer a scrap of criticism of her sibling and any sister worth her salt will rend him.

CHARLOTTE GRAY

My Guide

*She takes my hand and leads me along paths
I would not have dared explore alone.*

MAYA V. PATEL

*Thanks to birth order.... I have something
she'll never have: a powerhouse to be inspired by.*

PATRICIA VOLK ON HER SISTER JO ANN

... my sisters have shown me how to live.

GEORGETTE WASSERSTEIN, FROM "SISTERS"
BY CAROL SALINE AND SHARON WOHLMUTH

How could I be jealous of her? Everything she has she shares with me. I had a life-threatening illness.... I had just come out of a coma when she came to the hospital and leaned over my bed and whispered, "Little Mich, little Mich, don't you worry about anything. Wherever I go, I'll take care of you." And she has.

MICHIE NADER, SISTER OF KATIE LEE GIFFORD

A Sister Is Never Fooled!

Sisters don't need words.
They have perfected a language of snarls and smiles
and frowns and winks
– expressions of shocked surprise
and incredulity and disbelief.
Sniffs and snorts and gasps and sighs
– that can undermine
any tale you're telling.

PAM BROWN, b.1928

Every sister has a fund of embarrassing stories
she can bring out at the most effective moment.

PAMELA DUGDALE

Only a sister can compare the sleek body that now exists with the
chubby body hidden underneath. Only a sister knows about former
pimples, failing math, and underwear kicked under the bed.

LAURA TRACY, FROM "THE SECRET BETWEEN US"

A sister smiles when one tells one's stories –
for she knows where the decoration has been added.

CHRIS MONTAIGNE

she knows it all

Who sees to it
that my head
stays the
right size?

PAM BROWN, b.1928

Being with you, I can be completely myself. When it's just us, I can be myself and know you'll love and understand me no matter what. You don't want anything from me except my happiness.

CORETTA SCOTT KING,
IN A LETTER TO HER SISTER
EDYTHE

you'll

love

and

understand

me

For all the times you cleaned me up
before Mum saw me. For helping me remember
that awful nine times table. For officiating at my
canary's funeral.

For punching Herbert Johnson on the nose.

For sewing up the hem on my best party dress.

For reading "Pooh" when I had chicken-pox.

For teaching me to swim.

For driving away the bogey men.

For being my friend when no one else seemed to be.

Thank you.

PAM BROWN, b.1928

*W*e two have one beginning.
Slept and stirred in the same
enfolding dark,
our senses echoing the hushing of
one heart.
We tumbled into brightness, into
cold, into vast emptiness
– were gathered softly up,
nuzzled into safety.
Know the same scent and
touch of love.
Their sharing will outlast
all else.

PAM BROWN, b.1928

A sibling may be the sole
keeper of one's core identity, the
only person with the keys to
one's unfettered, more
fundamental self.

MARIAN SANDMAIER

SHARING THE GOOD NEWS

My sister Gigi is the first person I call
with good news, so we can celebrate together....
No matter what I'm feeling, her response is the one
I want to hear before anyone else's. She is my
sounding board, my confidante, my keeper of
secrets – and my best friend.

KATHLEEN O'KEEFE

What's the good of news
if you haven't a sister to share it?

JENNY DE VRIES

My sister Winifred only occasionally suggested that I was doing
the wrong thing, and looking back over the best part of a century,
I marvel at how a child so young could be so wise.
She never corrected me, she simply supplied me with information
regarding how things could be conveniently done, since it had
not come my way.
Now I had someone to walk with who would pick me up
if I fell and would pluck me back if I started to cross the road
without making sure it was clear.

DAME REBECCA WEST ON HER SISTER WINIFRED

Elder sisters all through history have always taken over when the need has arisen. In every time and place there is a skinny child stirring a pot, with a baby firmly hugged against her hip. Keeping one eye on her siblings sprawled across the floor. Telling a sulking youngster to get on with its chores. Listening to the shouts of laughter in the street. Struggling from the river with a slopping water pot. Trudging home from market with a laden basket. Hushing a restless infant into sleep. Counting the coins in a worn purse. Inspecting backs of necks and finger nails. Stitching holes in stockings. Blowing noses. Hauling unwilling children off to school.
A child old beyond her years.
A child deprived of childhood.

PAM BROWN, b.1928

Both within the family and without, our sisters hold up our mirrors: our images of who we are and of who we can dare to be.

ELIZABETH FISHEL

Who greets the news of your most incredible achievement with, "Good. I told you that you could do it?"

PAM BROWN

Sisters function as safety nets in a chaotic world simply by being there for each other.

CAROL SALINE, FROM "SISTERS"

As in so many life passages behind us and ahead of us, we've become reference points for each other; lodestars for each other, as we separate and cross paths again.

ELIZABETH FISHEL

It wouldn't have been like my sister to throw her arms around me the day our mother died, offering extravagant promises of undying approval and devotion. Always an unflinchingly honest person, she offered me the one promise she could wholeheartedly make. "I'm the only one now who remembers the day of your birth," she told me. "No matter what, I will always be your sister."

JOYCE MAYNARD, NOVELIST ABOUT HER SISTER RONA

... when, many years later,
she reminded me of some advice
I had given her when I was in college
that she had followed,
I realized the awesome power
and responsibility wielded
by the older sister.
She'd *treasured* what I said,
listened to the advice,
and remembered it years later;
I didn't think anyone
paid any attention to anything
I ever said!

SALLY R. ZANGER, ON HER SISTER ABBY

It's only in the last five years that I've truly learned how to love my sister with all my soul and at the very deepest possible level, without that crippling sense of competition. And to forgive her for all those school reports describing her as "pleasant and friendly", while mine just growled "disruptive influence!"

MOLLY PARKIN

I hated you so much sometimes.
The times you went off with your friends
and left me.
The times you got far better marks than mine.
The times you got new shoes and I didn't.
The times I had to wear your outgrown winter coat.
The times you got more birthday cards than me.
The times you had no fillings at the dentist
and I did.
… I envied you, your smile, your feet,
your sense of balance.
I thought Mum loved you best.
And it was years and years before I discovered that
you had envied me.

CHRIS MONTAIGNE

SEEING YOU AGAIN...

Every now and then our arms would fly around
each other in a hug and we'd look in each other's
eyes and say how happy we were.
We didn't have anything very original or profound
to say. We were both so excited we were almost
out of our minds.... We were overwhelmed at
finally getting to see each other.

BERNIECE BAKER MIRACLE, SISTER OF MARILYN MONROE

It was a vision of pleasure to see you; I've thought
of you fifty times each day – in fact you may be
said to be a kind of running bass....

VIRGINIA WOOLF (1882-1941),
FROM "THE LETTERS OF VIRGINIA WOOLF"

MUTUAL ADMIRATION!

LILLIAN GISH ON HER SISTER DOROTHY

She is laughter, even on the cloudy days of life; nothing bothers her or saddens her or concerns her lastingly.
... She is the side of me that God left out. Her funny stories, her delight in sitting on men's hats, her ability to interest herself in a hundred and one people... her talent for quick and warm friendships, her philosophy of silver linings....
The world to her is a big picnic with a great merry-go-round and lots of popcorn and wonderful balloons.

DOROTHY GISH ON HER SISTER LILLIAN

How I envy her the singleness of purpose, the indefatigability, the unabating seriousness which have taken her straight to the heights she has reached and will carry her on and on!
.. She is blessed with a constitution that can respond to any demand. Long after I am ready to be hauled off on a shutter, she, apparently so frail, can go on tirelessly, unruffled, cool and calm....
... She is to me a never-ending source of astonishment and admiration. And I never cease to wonder at my luck in having for my sister the woman who possesses all the qualities of greatness.

Often siblings don't see much of each other

once they've grown and gone — nor do they write

or telephone.

But their lives are inextricably entwined

and distance cannot dim their mutual concern.

When trouble comes all sibling rivalry is forgotten

and they give all their energies to comfort,

aid and rescue.

PAM BROWN, b.1928

Always, since we are chiquita,

our art very elaborate.

Our minds like cameras,

full of ideas.

One remember what

the other forget.

HAYDEE SCULL, FROM "SISTERS"
BY CAROL SALINE AND SHARON WOHLMUTH

[Having a sister is]

like having a best friend

around for your whole life.

AMANDA HECTOR, FROM "SISTERS"
BY CAROL SALINE AND SHARON WOHLMUTH

What sets sisters apart from brothers and also from friends is a very intimate meshing of heart, soul and the mystical cords of memory.

CAROL SALINE, FROM "SISTERS"

They say, "Never look back" –
but all we've done together, seen together,
been together is worth remembering.
All the sharing, all the daring.
All the mischief, all the fun.

PAM BROWN, b.1928

To the outside world we all grow old.
But not to brothers and sisters.
We know each other as we always were.
We know each other's hearts.
We share private family jokes.
We remember family feuds and secrets,
family griefs and joys.
We live outside the touch of time.

CLARA ORTEGA

Sisters are different. They heard the sobbing in the darkness.
They lived through all your triumphs, all your failures,
all your loves and losses. They have no delusions.
They lived with you too long.
And so, when you achieve some victory, friends are delighted –
but sisters hold your hands in silence and shine with happiness.
For they know the cost.

PAM BROWN, b.1928

Sisters know about each other's private self better than anyone
else ever will. Sisters sometimes talk about how they can see
through each other, never misled by the other's pretences,
instinctively knowing the other's true feelings. This form of
closeness gives a sister a potentially devastating power over the
other, but instead it is used to support and protect each other.

TARA WOODS, b.1971

Having a sister means having one of the most beautiful and unique of human relationships. We share with our sisters a special intimacy, a communion of heart and mind more powerful than any friendship.

AUTHOR UNKNOWN

We heard a song, we heard it in harmony.

MAXENE ANDREWS, ON THE ANDREWS SISTERS

How do people make it through life without a sister?

I need her as much as she needs me. She is my biggest security in life. We... share the same passions and hobbies, and we even fight like cats and dogs. Mary creates for me a sense of well-being beyond any relationship I have ever experienced. Without her, where would I be? It's a unique relationship. We share a soul.

SARA CORPENING, ABOUT HER TWIN SISTER MARY

Although we always professed that we wanted to be alone,
we needed each other as safeguards, bulwarks
against the world. We needed each other's physical connivance
in the events of our lives....

POLLY DEVLIN

My sister was no ordinary woman – no woman ever is, but to me, my sister less than any. When my mother had died, she, my sister, had become my mother, and more mother to me than any mother could ever have been. I was immensely proud of her. I shone in the reflection of her green-eyed, black-haired, gypsy beauty.... She was innocent and guileless and infinitely protectable. She was naïve to the point of saintliness, and wept a lot at the misery of others. She felt all tragedies except her own. I had read of the Knights of Chivalry and I knew that I had a bounden duty to protect her above all other creatures.

RICHARD BURTON (1925-1984), FROM "A CHRISTMAS STORY"

$\mathcal{D}$o you remember – the first glimpse of the sea?
The wavelets curling round the toes?
The corrugated sand? The search for stones?
And voices calling, "Tea!"
Wet hair, the peeling off of clinging bathing suits.
Wet towels and slopping pails of sea carried across
the stones and round the sprawling bodies to wash
our gritty feet? Sand in the socks, sand in the
sandwiches, sand on the chalet floor – and winkles
that escaped the jam jar set beside the bed?
Do you remember thinking we were lost? And
spotting Dad a dozen yards away?
And the last day. The last paddle.
The ritual shopping for the sticks of rock and
souvenir for Grandma.
The Greek Islands now. And St. Petersburg.
Wonderful.
But never quite the same as being with
you on the spree.

PAM BROWN, b.1928

Sisters. Yes, we're just sisters.
Our story is not heroic, not even
memorable. But when I need
support I sense you quietly by me.
I always will.

HELEN THOMSON, b.1943

Friends came and went. And lovers. Jobs and adventures.
Beliefs. Ambitions.
But there has been a constancy.
My love for you
and yours for me.

CHARLOTTE GRAY

Husbands come and go; children come and
eventually they go. Friends grow up and move away.
But the one thing that's never lost is your sister.

GAIL SHEENY, FROM "SISTERS"

Sisters are sisters forever and forever.

PAM BROWN, b.1928

Until the ending of our days, we will be part of one another's lives. However far apart, however different, we are essential to each other.

PAM BROWN, b.1928

When we were kids, we took it for granted that there was always a sister on the other end of the teeter-totter. Now I realize what that really means. How do people get through life if they have to go to a playground by themselves?

DONNA MASIEJCZYK, FROM "SISTERS"
BY CAROL SALINE AND SHARON WOHLMUTH

Nothing could ever come between us.

JACQUELINE KENNEDY ONASSIS, ON HER SISTER LEE

We can never be separate. She inside me. I inside her.
We always inside here, in the heart.

HAYDEE SCULL, FROM "SISTERS" BY CAROL SALINE AND SHARON WOHLMUTH

Sisters are connected throughout their lives by a special bond – whether they try to ignore it or not. For better or for worse, sisters remain sisters, until death do them part.

BRIGID McCONVILLE,
FROM "SISTERS: LOVE AND CONFLICT WITHIN THE LIFELONG BOND"

Most relationships – friendships, love affairs, marriages – require a certain amount of servicing to keep them ticking over. When a year or so passes without having heard from friends, people tend to say they have "lost touch". If couples so much as part to take a holiday, eyebrows tend to be raised, while most relatives expect the occasional phone call or Christmas card at least.

Yet the sisters' relationship seems to be a dramatic exception. For many sisters the bond which is forged in childhood is not only durable but it hardly requires any formal attention in the great gaps of time and space that often separate them in adult life. "Losing touch" generally isn't an issue.

BRIGID McCONVILLE,
FROM "SISTERS: LOVE AND CONFLICT WITHIN THE LIFELONG BOND"

We may look old and wise to the outside world.
But to each other, we are still in junior school.

CHARLOTTE GRAY

... if we believed in the media we would think the only significant
relationship in our lives is a romantic one. Yet sisterhood is probably
the one that will last longer than any other...
a sister will always be around.

JANE DOWDESWELL, FROM "SISTERS ON SISTERS"

Neither one of us ever married and we've lived together most all of our
lives, and probably know each other better than any
two human beings on Earth. After so long, we are in some ways like one
person. She is my right arm. If she were to die first, I'm not sure if I
would want to go on living because the reason I am living
is to keep her living.

SADIE DELANEY, AGED 103, ABOUT HER SISTER BESSIE, AGED 101
FROM "HAVING OUR SAY"

PICTURE CREDITS

page 7: **Sloe Blossom,** © 1998 William Stewart Macgeorge, Smith Art Gallery & Museum, Stirling, The Bridgeman Art Library.

page 9: **Children On The Beach,** Mary Cassatt, National Gallery of Washington, AISA.

pages 10/11: **Bathers,** Pierre Auguste Renoir, Christie's Images.

pages 12/13: **Ladies Knitting,** © 1998 Martha Walter, David David Gallery, Philadelphia, Superstock.

page 15: **The Song of the Children,** B. St Jersschantz, Galeria del Ateneum, Helsinki, AISA.

page 16: **Friends On The Beach,** © 1998 Dorothea Sharp, Whitford & Hughes, London, The Bridgeman Art Library.

page 18: **At The Seaside,** © 1998 Dorothea Sharp, John Davies Fine Paintings, The Bridgeman Art Library.

page 21: **The Little Needle Women,** Albert Anker, AKG London.

pages 22/23: **The Cotton Pickers,** Winslow Homer, Los Angeles County Museum of Art.

page 24: **It's Our Corner** (Portrait of the Painter's Daughters), Sir Lawrence Alma-Tadema, Giraudon/The Bridgeman Art Library.

page 26: **Children At The Seaside,** © 1998 Frank Gascoigne Heath, Bradford Art Galleries & Museums, The Bridgeman Art Library.

page 28: **Springtime,** Edward Atkinson Hornel, Sotheby's Transparency Library.

pages 30/31: **Women Leaning on a Fence,** Edgar Degas, Edimedia.

page 33: **The Picnic,** © 1998 James Faulds, Beaton-Brown Fine Paintings, London, The Bridgeman Art Library.

page 34: **Portrait of Two Girls,** Pierre Auguste Renoir, Musée de l'Orangerie, Paris,Giraudon/The Bridgeman Art Library.

page 37: **Tindera,** © 1998 Miranda Irineo, Private Collection.

page 39: **Wake Up! It's Christmas Morning!** © 1998 Arthur John Elsley, Fine Art Photographic Library.

page 41: **Springtime,** Alexander Mann, Whitford and Hughes, London, The Bridgeman Art Library.

pages 42/43: **Two Sisters,** J.F. Claustre, Archivi Alinari, Florence.

page 45: **At the Window,** © 1998 Peter Vilhelm Ilsted, Sotheby's Transparency Library.

pages 46/47: **The Chatterer,** Camille Pissarro, Messrs Wildenstein & Co., Ltd, Image Select International.

page 49: **Girl with Red Hat,** © 1998 Raphael Soyer, Thyssen-Bornemisza Collection, Madrid, Art Resource.

page 50: **The First Lesson,** Carl Larsson, Norrkoping Museum, Sweden, The Bridgeman Art Library.

page 52: **Brother and Sister,** © 1998 Adolf Fenyes, National Gallery, Budapest, Superstock.

page 54: **The Sisters,** Ralph Peacock, Image Select, London.

page 56: **The Gobelin,** Viktor Borisov-Musatov, Tretiakov Gallery, Moscow, Superstock.

page 59: **Women Combing Hair,** Edgar Degas, Private Collection.

page 61: **Children,** Valentin Serov, State Museum, St. Petersburg, Scala.

page 62: **Two Young Women Seated,** © 1998 William Henry Margetson, Bonhams, London, The Bridgeman Art Library.

page 64: **The Cherry Picker,** Berthe Morisot, Musée Marmottan, Paris, Giraudon.

page 67: **In The Orchard,** © 1998 Henry Herbert La Thangue, Bradford Art Galleries & Museums, The Bridgeman Art Library.

page 69: **Two Friends,** © 1998 Gerard Sekoto, Johannesburg Art Gallery, South Africa, The Bridgeman Art Library.

page 70: **At the Milliner,** Edgar Degas, Thyssen-Bornemisza Collection, Madrid, Art Resource.

page 73: **Young Girls At The Piano,** Pierre Auguste Renoir, Musée de l'Orangerie, Paris, William Walter Collection, Bulloz.

page 75: **Flower Sellers,** © 1998 Alfredo Ramos Martinez, Christie's Images, New York, Superstock.

page 77: **A Summer Evening,** Frederick Cayley Robinson, The Bridgeman Art Library.

page 78: **A Young Girl and Boy By The Fire,** © 1998 Marion Boyd Allen, Sotheby's Transparency Library.

pages 80/81: **A Day By The Sea,** © 1998 Dorothea Sharp, Waterman Fine Art Ltd, London, The Bridgeman Art Library.

pages 82/83: **Girls At The Piano,** Gabriel Deluc, Musée Bonnat, Bayonne, Giraudon.

page 84: **Waiting For The Tortillas,** © 1998 Diego Rivera, University of California, Index.

pages 86/87: **Fisher Girls By The Sea,** Winslow Homer, The Bridgeman Art Library.

page 89: **Summer Evening at the South Beach, Skagen,** Peder Severin Kroyer, The Hirschsprungske Collection, Copenhagen, The Bridgeman Art Library.

page 91: © 1998 Peter Fiore, Artworks.

TEXT CREDITS

BARBARA ALPERT: From *No Friend Like A Sister*, Ed. B. Alpert. © 1996, B. Alpert. Permission granted by The Berkley Publishing Group, a division of Penguin Putnam Inc. All rights reserved.

DIRK BOGARDE: From *An Orderly Man*, published by Chatto and Windus. © 1983 Labofilms. Used with permission of Random House UK Ltd and Alfred A. Knopf, Inc.

RICHARD BURTON: From *A Christmas Story*, published by Hodder Headline. Used with permission.

AMANDA HECTOR: Reprinted with permission from *Sisters*, essays by Carol Saline and photographs by Sharon J. Wohlmuth, © 1994, published by Running Press Book Publishers, Philadelphia and London.

ANNE MORROW LINDBERGH: From *Bring Me A Unicorn:* Diaries and Letters of Anne Morrow Lindbergh 1922-1928. © 1972 Anne Morrow Lindbergh, reprinted by permission of Harcourt Brace and Co. and Random House UK Ltd.

DONNA MASIEJCZYCK: Reprinted with permission from *Sisters*, essays by Carol Saline and photographs by Sharon J. Wohlmuth, © 1994, published by Running Press Book Publishers, Philadelphia and London.

BRIGID McCONVILLE: From *Sisters: Love and Conflict Within the Lifelong Bond*, published by Pan Macmillan Ltd. © 1985 B. McConville.

MOLLY PARKIN: From *Moll: The Making of Molly Parkin*, published by Gollancz. © 1993 Molly Parkin.

CAROL SALINE: Reprinted with permission from *Sisters*, essays by Carol Saline and photographs by Sharon J. Wohlmuth, © 1994, published by Running Press Book Publishers, Philadelphia and London.

HAYDEE SCULL: Reprinted with permission from *Sisters*, essays by Carol Saline and photographs by Sharon J. Wohlmuth, © 1994, published by Running Press Book Publishers, Philadelphia and London.

GAIL SHEENEY: Reprinted with permission from *Sisters*, essays by Carol Saline and photographs by Sharon J. Wohlmuth, © 1994, published by Running Press Book Publishers, Philadelphia and London.

DAME REBECCA WEST: From *Family Memories*, © 1987 The Estate of Rebecca West DBE. Used by permission of Viking Penguin, a division of Penguin Putnam, Inc.

VIRGINIA WOOLF: From *Letters of Virginia Woolf*, Volume: 1936-1941 by Joanna Trautmann and Nigel Nicolson. Published by The Hogarth Press. © 1980 Quentin Bell and Angelica Garnett, reprinted by permission of Harcourt Brace & Co.

GEORGETTE WASSERSTEIN: Reprinted with permission from *Sisters*, essays by Carol Saline and photographs by Sharon J. Wohlmuth, © 1994, published by Running Press Book Publishers, Philadelphia and London.